First edition 2005
Printed in Canada

by Mauro Golmarvi
Recipes developed by Mauro Golmarvi and Iram Macias
Assaggio recipe editing by Iris Gannon
Food Photographer: Angie Norwood Browne
Food Stylist: Patty Wittmann
Photographers: Angie Norwood Browne and Jaimie Trueblood
Editorial Director: Petyr Beck
Editors: Judy Gouldthorpe and Hillary Self
Designer: Nancy Gellos
Publisher: Barry Provorse

Library of Congress Cataloguing-in-Publication Data

Golmarvi, Mauro. 1958—
Assaggio ristorante cookbook : Mauro's passion / Mauro Golmarvi ; recipes by Mauro Golmarvi, Iram Macias ; photos by Angie Norwood Browne, Jaimie Trueblood.
p. cm.
Includes index.
ISBN 1-933245-00-X
1. Cookery, Italian. 2. Assaggio (Restaurant) I. Macias, Iram. II. Assaggio (Restaurant) III. Title.
TX723.G62927 2005
641.5945—dc22
2005011992

Published by
Documentary Media LLC
3250 41st Avenue SW
Seattle, Washington 98116
(206) 935-9292
email: books@docbooks.com
www.documentarymedia.com

Table of Contents

Introduction

FOOD OF PASSION

To taste the passion is to get to the heart of eating and cooking. It's not about fancy spices or complicated dishes; it's about simplicity, honesty, and the freshest ingredients you can find. But most of all, it is about passion. To cook with passion is to create food for the soul. What's the secret? You have to let yourself be inspired, to care, to enjoy the process: it's not sex, it's making love.

I have been forming this cookbook in my mind for years, always simmering it, perfecting it, slow-cooking it in my imagination, waiting for the right time to bring it to the table. Why is now the right time? Because more and more, people are beginning to understand the connection between food and the soul. Because today we are so fortunate to have local fresh ingredients to work with. It is the perfect condition for food of passion! This book is not about cooking like a chef. It's about you and me with a few friends, at home, drinking wine, getting happy, and cooking. Your kitchen is the center of the passion.

When people ask me, "How did you learn to cook?" I tell them that my stove and my oven are my masters: they teach me everything; they are like my gods. They are not fancy, but they are mine, and they allow me to express the passion of cooking. The point is not to make your home kitchen like a restaurant kitchen. It should be the other way around!

But most of all, it is about passion.

For a while, everyone was publishing cookbooks, but very few of them were inspiring or useful. Very few Italian cookbooks have anything to do with Italian food. I get worked up about this! One of the most meaningful compliments I have ever received was when Stefano Bonilli, one of the founders of the Slow Food movement and editor of *Gambero Rosso* (the most prestigious restaurant guide in Italy), wrote in his column in the Italian newspaper *Corriere della Sera*, "If you go to America, you have to go to Assaggio Ristorante in Seattle to taste the passion." What I want to do in this book is to share what I have learned in my life about food. To help people create food for the soul.

Cooking is the center-point of everything that is important to me. When I sit at the table with my daughter Francesca before school, we eat, we talk, and we focus on each other. Given our busy lives, this time with her is very special. My family life revolves around cooking. It's so important to savor your kitchen and table time, enjoy every bite. I feel the same way about my restaurant. When you come into Assaggio, I want to share that with you, make food for your soul, allow you to enjoy every bite. My greatest hope is that with this cookbook, you can take that philosophy into your own home.

Many of the recipes we have included in this cookbook have been favorites at Assaggio over the years, some have won awards, and some are recent additions to our menu. My goal has been to keep it fresh, simple, and honest so that you can be creative, improvise, and let the passion take over. You have to be sensitive to the season and what ingredients are fresh so you can let that guide you. In wintertime don't insist on fresh figs just because you can get greenhouse-flown-in-from-wherever fruit. No, you're a criminal! You should be arrested! Prepare your fig salad in August or September, when they are straight from the trees.

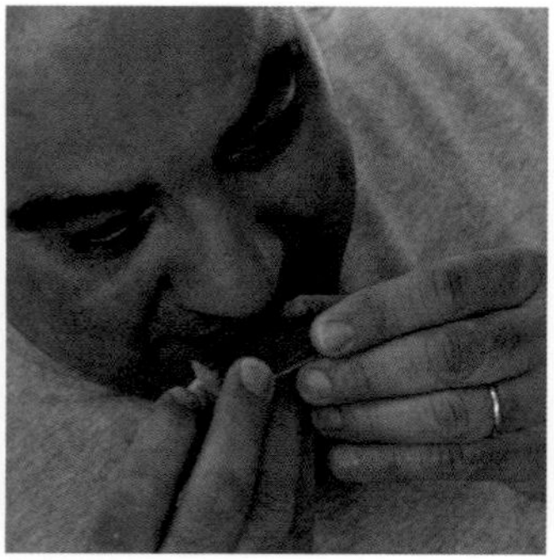

It's the quality of ingredients that makes the dish honest.

If you don't find the exact herb, fish, or cut of meat, don't worry! It's the quality of ingredients that makes the dish honest. The passion starts when you are shopping. No fresh halibut? You love cod, and the cod looks great today, so use cod — it's okay! You can relax because you cared enough to find the freshest ingredients.

Let your imagination and desires inspire you. Let the ingredients themselves inspire you. If in the morning I'm standing on my deck drinking my coffee, and I am looking out over the water of Puget Sound, believe me, I'm going to cook seafood for you tonight. Let something get into your mind, into your nose, be ready for anything!

1
Antipasto

Nobody should start a meal without an antipasto. A small dish of something special gets you started, gets you in the mood, it makes you want more. There are no limits to what you might serve as an antipasto; it can be simple or complex. You don't need much, a mouthful or two for each guest, but it is a very important first bite, like the first kiss. So it's a law. You have to have antipasti.

Using fresh ingredients doesn't just mean using fresh herbs instead of dried, although that's important. Using fresh ingredients also means using what is in season. When the tomatoes in your yard start getting ripe in the late summer and fall, that's when you should make the caprese. Don't insist on caprese in the wintertime — it's criminal; I mean, you can't do those things. You can't have wild boar in the middle of the summer or wild mushrooms in the early summer. You can't! Wait for the season. There are so many good foods, and you have to give each of them the time they deserve. Don't rush the seasons and try to cook with ingredients that aren't ready yet. Enjoy each of them as much as you can while they're fresh. And when one is done, something else is coming into season, and you can move on to other dishes.

You have to use what you find in your garden. My wife went out to the garden one day, and she gathered so many tomatoes up in her shirt. And she said, "How are we going to eat them?" I said, "Let's dry some of them." I cut them in half, put them in the oven overnight on low heat, and I made the best sun-dried tomatoes out of them. But fresh sun-dried tomatoes — not dry like beef jerky. And then, we had a lot of mushrooms. And I said, "We have to do something about these mushrooms." So we started doing chanterelles over veal chops. And for the side dish, we took a half big cut of tomato, baked it in the oven, and then broiled bread crumbs with Parmigiano-Reggiano on top until the topping was golden. It was the best dinner.

Calamari Saltati

SAUTÉED CALAMARI

2 tablespoons olive oil
2 garlic cloves, minced
1 tablespoon chopped fresh rosemary
12 ounces calamari, cleaned and sliced into rings
1/4 teaspoon salt
1/4 teaspoon freshly ground black pepper
2 Italian plum tomatoes, diced
1 1/2 tablespoons chopped fresh Italian parsley
1/2 cup dry white wine
2 tablespoons balsamic vinegar
3 tablespoons dried bread crumbs

This dish can be saved and served over pasta the next day.

Heat olive oil in a medium sauté pan over high heat. Add garlic and sauté until golden brown. Stir in rosemary. Add calamari, salt, and pepper and stir. Add tomatoes and stir for 1 minute. Add 1 tablespoon parsley, wine, and vinegar; stir and cook for about 2 minutes. Stir in 2 1/2 tablespoons bread crumbs.

Transfer to a serving plate. Garnish with remaining bread crumbs and parsley.

Serves 4.

Pinot Grigio
Pinot Gris

Gamberoni Saltati
SAUTÉED PRAWNS

2 ounces goat cheese, crumbled
3 tablespoons fresh lemon juice
Pinch of chopped fresh mint
2 tablespoons water
2 teaspoons balsamic vinegar
2 tablespoons extra-virgin olive oil
1 pound (16 to 20) wild Gulf prawns, peeled and deveined
Salt
Freshly ground black pepper
1 cup mixed salad greens
2 lemons, cut into wedges

Combine goat cheese, lemon juice, mint, water, and vinegar in a saucepan. Stir and cook over medium heat until creamy.

Heat olive oil in a medium sauté pan over medium heat. Sauté prawns, adding salt and pepper to taste.

Divide salad greens among 4 plates. Dip prawns in the sauce and arrange around the salad on each plate. Garnish with lemon wedges.

Serves 4.

Soave
Riesling

Caponata

1/4 cup olive oil
2 large carrots, peeled and cut into 1/4-inch pieces
2 stalks celery, cut into 1/4-inch pieces
1 medium onion, cut into 1/4-inch pieces
1/4 cup chopped mixed fresh Italian herbs
(1 sprig each of rosemary, thyme, and oregano and 3 sage leaves)
1/2 teaspoon salt
1/2 teaspoon freshly ground black pepper
2 tablespoons sugar
2 garlic cloves, minced
1 28-ounce can peeled plum tomatoes, chopped or mashed
1/2 cup white wine vinegar
4 small or 2 large eggplants, skin on, cut into 1/4- to 1/2-inch cubes
1 cup water
3 tablespoons capers in brine
1 cup kalamata olives, pitted and sliced
2 teaspoons chopped fresh Italian parsley

Heat olive oil in a large saucepan over medium heat. Stir in carrots, celery, and onion and cook for 4 minutes, or until onion begins to soften. Stir in fresh herbs, salt, pepper, and sugar and cook for 2 minutes. Add garlic and cook, stirring, for 2 minutes.

Add tomatoes and vinegar and cook over medium heat for several minutes, until the mixture begins to boil. Stir in eggplant and water and increase the heat to high. Cook, covered, for 10 minutes, then reduce the heat to medium. Add capers and olives, cover, and cook for another 10 minutes. Carrots should be soft but not mushy.

Transfer to a serving bowl or platter and sprinkle with parsley.
Serve hot or at room temperature.

Serves 4 to 6.

Barbera
Pinot Noir

Caprese
TOMATO AND MOZZARELLA

4 ripe Italian plum tomatoes
6 ounces fresh buffalo mozzarella
8 to 10 fresh basil leaves
1/3 cup extra-virgin olive oil
Freshly ground black pepper
Salt

Cut tomatoes into 1/4-inch-thick slices. Cut mozzarella into 1/4-inch-thick slices.

On 4 individual salad plates, layer tomato, basil leaf, then mozzarella; repeat with a second layer. Drizzle with olive oil, a generous dash of pepper, and salt to taste. For an alternative presentation, arrange on a serving plate.

Serves 4.

Chardonnay
Sauvignon Blanc

Carciofi Fritti
FRIED ARTICHOKES

4 large artichokes
2 lemons, 1 halved and 1 cut into wedges
4 extra-large eggs
1/2 teaspoon salt
1/2 teaspoon freshly ground black pepper
1 cup unbleached all-purpose flour
1 quart vegetable oil
1/4 cup extra-virgin olive oil
Lemon Dressing

Clean and trim artichokes and cut vertically, including the stem in the center, into slices about 1/2 inch thick. Place artichoke pieces in a large bowl of cold water; squeeze the juice from 2 lemon halves into the bowl and let stand for 30 minutes.

Line a serving dish with paper towels.

Beat eggs with a pinch of salt in a small bowl. Drain the artichoke pieces, dry with paper towels, then sprinkle with salt and pepper. Place artichoke pieces in a colander, sprinkle with flour, and shake to coat. The pieces will be lightly coated and the excess flour will drop through.

Heat vegetable oil and olive oil in a heavy frying pan to 375°F. Dip each artichoke piece in the egg mixture and place in the hot oil. Deep-fry until golden, about 2 minutes on each side. Remove cooked artichoke pieces from the frying pan with a strainer/skimmer and place on the serving dish to drain. Repeat the procedure for all artichoke pieces.

To serve, remove paper towels from the serving dish, drizzle artichokes with Lemon Dressing, and garnish with lemon wedges.

Serves 4.

Salsa di Limone
LEMON DRESSING

Juice of 2 lemons
1/2 cup extra-virgin olive oil
1/2 teaspoon salt
1/2 teaspoon freshly ground black pepper
1 tablespoon chopped fresh Italian parsley

In a small bowl, combine all ingredients and whisk thoroughly.

Roero Arneis
Sauvignon Blanc

Vongole Oreganato

SAUTÉED CLAMS WITH OREGANO

2 teaspoons extra-virgin olive oil
4 garlic cloves, minced
2 pounds fresh clams, scrubbed and rinsed
under cold running water
1 cup dry white wine
1 teaspoon dried oregano
2 lemons
6 fresh basil leaves, chopped

Heat olive oil and garlic in a large sauté pan over high heat. When garlic is golden brown, add clams. Sauté for about 2 minutes. Add wine and oregano. Squeeze juice from lemons into the pan. Cover and cook for about 3 minutes, or until all the clams have opened. Transfer to a large serving dish, discarding any unopened clams. Sprinkle basil over the top and serve immediately.

Serves 4.

Verdicchio
Sauvignon Blanc

Salsiccia e Lenticchie
SAUSAGE AND LENTILS

Sauce:
4 tablespoons olive oil
2 garlic cloves, minced
1/2 teaspoon salt
1/2 teaspoon freshly ground black pepper
1 tablespoon chopped fresh rosemary
2 roasted red bell peppers, from a jar packed in olive oil or freshly roasted in the oven
Juice of 1 lemon

Lentil Mixture:
5 cups chicken broth (see recipe, page 61)
3 tablespoons olive oil
2 celery stalks, diced into 1/4-inch pieces
1 carrot, peeled and diced into 1/4-inch pieces
1 small onion, cut into 1/4-inch pieces
14 ounces (just under 2 cups) dried black or green lentils
1/2 teaspoon salt
1/2 teaspoon freshly ground black pepper
1 to 2 fresh sage leaves, torn

Sausage:
1 pound medium spicy Italian bulk sausage
1 egg
1 tablespoon chopped fresh Italian parsley
1/4 cup diced yellow onion

Garnish: chopped fresh Italian parsley

Sauce:
Combine 2 tablespoons olive oil, garlic, salt, pepper, and rosemary in a medium sauté pan. Cook over medium-low heat until garlic is golden brown. Transfer to a food processor; add roasted peppers, lemon juice, and 2 tablespoons olive oil. Puree, and set sauce aside.

Lentil Mixture:
Place chicken broth in a saucepan and bring to a boil.

Meanwhile, heat olive oil in a large frying pan over medium heat. Add celery, carrots, and onion; sauté for 3 minutes. Add lentils, salt, pepper, and sage. Sauté for 5 minutes, stirring.

Add 2 cups hot broth to the lentil mixture, stir, and cook over low heat for about 4 minutes. Cover and simmer until the liquid is absorbed, about 10 minutes. Add another 2 cups broth, cover, and simmer for about 5 minutes. Add remaining broth, cover, and continue to simmer for 5 minutes, or until the liquid has almost completely soaked into the lentils, which should be firm and just cooked through.

Sausage:
In a medium bowl, mix sausage, egg, parsley, and onion. Form sausage mixture into 6 patties about 3 to 4 inches across and 1/2 inch thick. Grill the patties (or sauté in a pan with olive oil) 4 to 5 minutes per side.

Spoon the lentil mixture onto plates and place the sausage patties on top. Pour the sauce over the patties, about 3 to 4 tablespoons per plate, sprinkle with parsley, and serve.

Serves 6.

Chianti
Cabernet Sauvignon

Funghi Saltati
SAUTÉED WILD MUSHROOMS

2 tablespoons olive oil
4 garlic cloves, minced
1 pound wild mushrooms, cleaned and sliced
1 sprig rosemary
3 tablespoons thinly sliced fresh basil leaves
1/2 cup red table wine
1/4 cup balsamic vinegar
6 sprigs fresh Italian parsley, finely chopped
(about 2 tablespoons)

Heat olive oil in a medium sauté pan over medium heat. Add garlic and sauté until golden brown. Add mushrooms and sauté for 5 minutes, or until lightly browned. Add rosemary and basil; reduce heat and simmer for 5 minutes. Add wine and vinegar; simmer for 5 minutes, or until the juices are reduced a little. Remove to a serving bowl, garnish with parsley, and serve with good bread and olive oil.

Verdicchio
Sauvignon Blanc

Serves 6.

You can also prepare this dish as crostini. Slice and toast artisan Italian bread, top with the mushroom relish, splash with olive oil, and sprinkle with parsley.

Portobello alla Griglia

GRILLED PORTOBELLO MUSHROOMS

1/2 cup balsamic vinegar
1/2 cup vegetable oil
2 teaspoons minced fresh rosemary
4 large fresh portobello mushrooms, brushed clean and stems removed
4 cups assorted salad greens, torn
Balsamic Vinaigrette
3 tablespoons crumbled Gorgonzola cheese
2 tablespoons crushed toasted walnuts

In a small bowl, stir together vinegar, vegetable oil, and rosemary. Divide between two large zipper-lock plastic bags. Place 2 mushrooms in each bag and seal; turn several times to coat evenly. Let stand at room temperature for 1 hour.

Prepare a fire in a covered grill. Place mushrooms on the grill rack, cover, and open the vents. Grill, turning once, until moist on the underside and just firm to the touch on the top, 3 to 4 minutes on each side. Remove from the grill.

Add greens to the bowl with Balsamic Vinaigrette and toss well. Divide among individual plates. Cut mushrooms into slices about 1 inch thick. Arrange mushrooms around tossed greens and top with Gorgonzola and walnuts.

Serves 4.

Vinaigrette Balsamico

BALSAMIC VINAIGRETTE

1 teaspoon Dijon mustard
3 tablespoons red wine vinegar
1/3 cup balsamic vinegar
1 teaspoon dried oregano
1 teaspoon dried rosemary
1 garlic clove, minced
1/2 teaspoon salt
1/2 teaspoon freshly ground black pepper
1/2 cup extra-virgin olive oil

In a large bowl, whisk together mustard, red wine vinegar, balsamic vinegar, oregano, rosemary, garlic, salt, and pepper. Slowly whisk in olive oil. This can be kept in a covered container in the refrigerator for up to 1 week.

Sangiovese
Pinot Noir

You have to use what you find in your garden.

2
Insalata

It is essential to use the freshest ingredients when preparing salads. If the apples are mealy or the greens are wilted, the salad will not be a success. If you wait until the apples and pears are just picked, each bite will delight you. But if you go to the store to collect the ingredients and they don't look good, substitute ingredients that do look good. That's the great thing about salads — you have a lot of room to substitute one fruit for another, one green for another.

Use the best olive oil you can get when you make your salads, as it is an important part of the flavor. It gives the salad that buttery taste and succulent texture; it looks great on the lips, important for dinner for lovers, dinner for the first date, things like that. Then they get closer and move in together soon . . . it's all in the olive oil.

Be very picky about your greens. Go for the organic. Steal a leaf at the market and taste it when they aren't looking. Arugula has many different variations of flavor. It's important to use fresh baby arugula in the Insalata Arugula because it has a more subtle flavor that goes well with Parmesan and prosciutto.

The salad is the most versatile part of a meal; it plays many roles in food of passion. I love to serve the salad after the main course rather than before. It's like cuddling. In the summer, the salad can be the main course itself. Always be open to serving your salad at different stages of your meal, and then go with what your heart tells you.

Insalata di Francesca

APPLE, PEAR, MIXED GREENS, AND CANDIED PISTACHIO SALAD

1 red apple, cored and diced
1 green apple, cored and diced
1 firm pear, cored and diced
4 ounces Gorgonzola cheese, crumbled
4 ounces Candied Pistachios
1 pound Italian mixed greens
Balsamic Vinaigrette (see recipe, page 31)

Combine ingredients in a large bowl and toss with vinaigrette to coat.

Serves 4.

I created this salad when my wife was pregnant with our daughter, Francesca. She was having cravings, so I picked an apple from the tree in our yard. It was tart, so I put a little lemon on it and got the idea to add sweet nuts to it. But how to sweeten pistachios? Honey tastes wonderful, but it's a bit sticky. Then I heated water and sugar so I could control the sweetness. Powdered sugar works well.

Pistacchio Dolce

CANDIED PISTACHIOS

3 cups water
1 cup raw, unsalted shelled pistachio nuts
1/3 cup confectioners' sugar or honey
3 tablespoons vegetable oil

Bring water to a boil in a medium saucepan. Have a colander ready near the sink. Add pistachios to the boiling water and blanch for 1 minute, then pour into the colander and rinse with cold tap water to cool. Transfer pistachios to a medium bowl. Add sugar or honey and stir to combine well.

Heat oil in a small to medium sauté pan over medium-high heat. When the oil starts to smoke, pour in the pistachio/sugar mixture and cook, stirring often. As the moisture cooks out, the pistachios will begin to turn light brown. Before they get too dark, pour the pistachios into a metal colander and then shake out onto a plate. Once they have cooled and hardened, you can break apart any pieces that are stuck together.

Barbera
Pinot Noir

Makes 1 cup.

This salad, named after my daughter, won the Best Taste Award at the 1998 Bite of Seattle.

Insalata di Panzanella

BREAD SALAD

1/2 pound Tuscan-style dark bread, lightly grilled or toasted and cut into 1/2- to 3/4-inch cubes
6 Roma tomatoes, cut into 1/2- to 3/4-inch cubes
1 pound fresh mozzarella, cut into 1/2- to 3/4-inch cubes
1/2 cup diced red onion
2 garlic cloves, minced
1/3 cup thinly sliced fresh basil
1 tablespoon finely chopped fresh Italian parsley
1/4 cup extra-virgin olive oil
3 tablespoons cold water
1/2 teaspoon salt
1/2 teaspoon freshly ground black pepper

In a large nonreactive bowl, combine bread, tomatoes, mozzarella, onion, garlic, basil, and parsley. Stir in olive oil, water, salt, and pepper. Mix ingredients well with your hands. Let stand for 20 minutes.

Chardonnay
Sauvignon Blanc

Serves 4.

One of my customers asked me if I could create a bread salad like one she had tasted on a trip to Italy. I said, "No problem." I had no idea what I was starting that day — the dish became very popular at the restaurant. But remember, traditionally this is a summer dish made with freshly grown tomatoes. And it has to be made with old bread. Set it out on top of your refrigerator for a couple of days. At the restaurant we cut the bread into slices and grill it lightly for texture and aroma.

Rucola con Fico e Prosciutto
ARUGULA SALAD WITH FIG AND PROSCIUTTO

8 fresh black figs, cut in half lengthwise
8 ounces fresh baby arugula
4 ounces Gorgonzola cheese, crumbled
1/3 cup walnuts, toasted and crushed
2 ounces thinly sliced prosciutto di Parma, cut into small strips

Dressing:
1/2 cup orange juice
1/2 cup balsamic vinegar
1 1/2 tablespoons extra-virgin olive oil
2 one-pint baskets of fresh black figs, or 20 dried Mission figs, cut in half lengthwise
Salt
Freshly ground black pepper

Grill fig halves lightly until marks begin to show; set aside.

To make the dressing, combine orange juice, vinegar, olive oil, and figs in a blender. Blend until smooth. Add salt and pepper to taste, then blend briefly. Unused dressing can be stored in a covered container in the refrigerator for up to a week.

Wash and dry arugula, then combine in a medium salad bowl with Gorgonzola, walnuts, and prosciutto. Toss with dressing to coat. Place on individual salad plates and garnish with grilled fig halves.

Pinot Nero
Pinot Noir

Serves 4.

Using fresh ingredients also means using what is in season.

Rucola con Prosciutto
ARUGULA SALAD WITH PROSCIUTTO

2 tablespoons fresh lemon juice
3 tablespoons extra-virgin olive oil
1/2 teaspoon salt
1/4 teaspoon freshly ground black pepper
1 pound baby arugula, preferably organic
16 thin slices prosciutto di Parma
Parmigiano-Reggiano cheese, shaved into 16 wide, thin slices
1 tablespoon chopped fresh Italian parsley

Chill 4 salad plates in the refrigerator.

In a small bowl, make a vinaigrette by mixing lemon juice, 2 tablespoons olive oil, salt, and pepper.

Place arugula in a large bowl. Add vinaigrette and toss well. Pile arugula in the center of the chilled salad plates. Arrange 4 prosciutto slices in an X-pattern over each serving of arugula. Top with slices of Parmigiano-Reggiano. Drizzle salads with remaining olive oil and sprinkle with parsley.

Serves 4.

Franciacorta
Blanc de Blancs

At the restaurant, we garnish each plate with crisp thin breadsticks.

The point is not to make your home kitchen like a restaurant kitchen. It should be the other way around.

3
Zuppa

Remember, what's important is the personality of the recipe and the honesty of the cooking. That means do not put twenty ingredients in one dish because how can you taste all of them? Too much fusion is confusion. Just do quality shopping and create a dish honestly. Nothing to hide with too much spice. Nothing that looks fussy. You don't have to go deep into the forest to find one leaf; forget about it!

You come to my house, and you see sea salt, kosher salt, and the best olive oil I can find. People keep fifty jars of dried herbs and spices in their cupboards for so long, but they don't get better with age. Not in my house. Take olive oil: the longer you keep it, the worse it gets. Use it. Enjoy it. It's not like wine. It doesn't get better with age.

Fresh herbs can make all the difference in soups, and they are available for most of the year. Whenever it's possible, find fresh basil, rosemary, and Italian parsley. The flavor is so much better, and it adds more to the soup than dried herbs.

On the other hand, with wintertime soups, it's good to use canned tomatoes; it's honest. Italians have always made winter minestrones with the tomatoes they canned last summer.

I am proud to share my broth and saffron tea recipes with you. At the restaurant we make these from scratch on a daily basis. Soups, pastas, and risottos are best when made with homemade stocks or broths. It's easy if you get into the habit of making a stock whenever you have beef, veal, or chicken bones left over from a dish you are cooking. Then store the stock in a sealed container in the fridge (for up to a week) or freezer for later use.

Minestrone
VEGETABLE SOUP

3 tablespoons extra-virgin olive oil
1 medium potato, peeled and cut into 1/4-inch cubes
2 large carrots, peeled and cut into 1/4-inch slices
1 medium onion, cut into 1/4-inch slices
2 celery stalks, cut into 1/4-inch slices
1 garlic clove, minced
1 zucchini, cut into 1/4-inch cubes
2 cups diced green beans
1 eggplant, diced
3 broccoli crowns, diced
1 sprig fresh oregano, chopped
1 sprig fresh rosemary, chopped
1 sprig fresh thyme, chopped
1 cup dry white wine
5 cups vegetable or chicken broth (see recipes, pages 60 and 61), or water
1 28-ounce can peeled, chopped tomatoes
Salt
Freshly ground black pepper

In a medium pot, combine olive oil, potato, carrots, onion, celery, and garlic. Stir and cook over medium heat for 5 minutes. Add zucchini, green beans, eggplant, and broccoli. Stir and cook for 2 minutes. Add oregano, rosemary, thyme, wine, broth, and tomatoes. Bring to a boil, stirring, then reduce heat, cover, and simmer for 45 minutes, stirring occasionally. Season with salt and pepper to taste.

Serves 4.

Barbera
Pinot Noir

Zuppa di Fagioli
BEAN SOUP

2 cups dried cannellini beans
4 tablespoons olive oil
1 small slice prosciutto rind, diced into 1/4-inch pieces
1 small red onion, cut into 1/4-inch pieces
1 medium potato, peeled and cut into 1/4-inch cubes
2 large garlic cloves, minced
1/4 cup red table wine
10 cups water or veal broth (see recipe, page 57)
1 cup canned tomatoes, preferably imported Italian, drained
1/2 teaspoon salt
1/2 teaspoon freshly ground black pepper
6 heaping teaspoons grated Parmigiano-Reggiano cheese

Place beans in a bowl and add enough cold water to cover by about 1 1/2 inches. Let soak overnight.

The next day, combine 2 tablespoons olive oil, prosciutto, onion, and potato in a medium stockpot. Cook over medium heat very gently until golden brown, then add garlic. Reduce heat to a simmer, add wine, and cook until reduced by half.

Drain the beans and add to the pot with the water or veal broth and tomatoes. Cover and simmer over low heat for about 45 minutes, or until the beans are cooked, being careful not to overcook. Stir in salt and pepper.

To serve, garnish with Parmigiano-Reggiano and remaining olive oil.

Serves 6.

Cannonau
Merlot

Zuppa di Pomodori

TOMATO SOUP

6 tablespoons olive oil, plus more for garnish
3 tablespoons minced onion
1 teaspoon chopped garlic
2 tablespoons finely chopped fresh Italian parsley
1/2 teaspoon finely chopped fresh rosemary
1 28-ounce can whole peeled tomatoes with juice
1/2 cup dry white wine
3 cups chicken or vegetable broth (see recipes, pages 61 and 60)
1/2 teaspoon salt
1/2 teaspoon freshly ground black pepper
4 thick slices of Tuscan bread, cut into 1-inch cubes
4 fresh basil leaves

Heat 6 tablespoons olive oil in a heavy-bottomed pan or earthenware pot over medium heat. Add onion and sauté until soft and translucent. Add garlic, parsley, and rosemary, and continue to sauté for about 2 minutes. Reduce heat, add tomatoes and wine, and simmer until wine is reduced by half. Add broth, salt, and pepper. Continue to simmer, partially covered, for about 20 minutes.

Remove from heat and stir in cubed bread. Cover and let stand for 3 minutes. Pour mixture into a food mill and puree. Return to medium heat for 3 minutes, or until heated through.

To serve, garnish with basil leaves and olive oil.

Serves 4.

Morellino
Merlot

Brodetto Anconetano

SEAFOOD SOUP

1 pound small to medium-sized mussels
1 pound clams
2 tablespoons butter
1/2 teaspoon salt
1/2 teaspoon freshly ground black pepper
1/2 pound squid, cut into rings
1/2 cup chopped green onions
1/2 cup saffron tea (see recipe, page 62)
2 cups fish broth (see recipe, page 60)
1 cup heavy cream
1/2 pound bay scallops
1/2 pound cooked, shelled bay shrimp
Fresh parsley leaves

Wash and scrub mussels and clams well under cold running water, discarding any open clams and mussels. Remove the beard from the mussels.

Melt butter over medium-low heat in a large saucepan; add salt and pepper. Add squid and sauté for 2 minutes. Add mussels and green onions and sauté for another 2 minutes. Pour in saffron tea, fish broth, and cream. Increase heat to medium, cover, and bring to a boil, about 5 minutes. Add clams and scallops, cover, and cook for 2 minutes. Stir in shrimp, cover, and cook for 2 more minutes, or until all clams have opened. Transfer immediately to a large, low-sided serving bowl, discarding any unopened mussels and clams.

Garnish with parsley leaves and serve with grilled Tuscan bread.

Serves 6.

Soave
Chardonnay

Zuppa di Lenticchie
LENTIL SOUP

1 1/2 cups dried lentils
2 small carrots, peeled and cut into 1/4-inch cubes
1 medium onion, finely chopped
2 celery stalks, cut into 1/4-inch slices
1 bay leaf
2 large garlic cloves, finely chopped
3 fresh sage leaves, finely chopped
1 heaping tablespoon finely chopped fresh rosemary
1/2 teaspoon salt
1/2 teaspoon freshly ground black pepper
4 tablespoons extra-virgin olive oil

Place lentils in a bowl and add enough cold water to cover by about 1 1/2 inches. Let soak for 3 hours.

Drain lentils and place in a medium saucepan with carrots, onion, celery, bay leaf, and garlic. Add enough cold water to cover lentils by about 2 inches. Cover and cook over low heat for about 45 minutes, or until nearly tender. Discard bay leaf. Add sage and rosemary and continue cooking, covered, for about 5 minutes. The lentils should be very soft and will begin to disintegrate. Add salt and pepper.

Drizzle with olive oil and serve hot.

Serves 4 to 6.

Sagrantino
Syrah

Brodo di Carne

BEEF OR VEAL BROTH

2 pounds beef or veal with bones (neck, shoulder, short ribs, brisket, various cuts of lean meat)
1 spongy bone (knee)
1 2 1/2-inch piece of bone marrow (optional)
2 celery stalks, with leaves, broken into 3 pieces
2 medium carrots, peeled and cut in half
1 medium onion, quartered
6 sprigs fresh Italian parsley
3 bay leaves, broken into small pieces
6 black peppercorns
2 tablespoons salt
2 tablespoons tomato paste (optional)
4 quarts plus 2 cups cold water

Rinse the bones quickly under cold running water. Place meat and bones in a very large pot. Add celery, carrots, onion, parsley, bay leaves, peppercorns, salt, and tomato paste. Add cold water and simmer, uncovered, over medium-low heat for 3 hours. Skim surface foam occasionally with a slotted spoon. More salt can be added at this point to taste.

Strain broth, discarding solids. Broth can be separated into convenient containers and frozen for later use.

Makes 3 to 4 quarts.

Zuppa di Melanzane
EGGPLANT SOUP

2 small eggplants
2 tablespoons olive oil, plus more for brushing
3 garlic cloves, peeled
1 cup onion cut into 1/4-inch slices
1 medium or 2 small potatoes, peeled and diced
1/3 cup dry white wine
2 cups chicken broth (see recipe, page 61) or water
2 cups heavy cream

Garnish: fresh sage leaves fried in olive oil, freshly shaved Parmesan cheese

Preheat oven to 400°F.

Cut eggplants in half lengthwise. Place skin side down on a sheet pan, brush with olive oil, and bake for 10 minutes. Brush garlic with olive oil and place in the pan with the eggplant. Continue baking until the eggplant and garlic are tender, about 20 minutes. Scrape the insides from the eggplant skins and discard skins.

In a 3-quart pot combine 2 tablespoons olive oil, eggplant, garlic, onion, and potato; cook, uncovered, over medium heat until the potato is tender. Add wine, reduce heat, and simmer for 10 minutes. Stir in chicken broth (or water) and cream; continue to simmer for 5 minutes. Pour the mixture into a blender and puree. Return to the pot and cook on low heat until slightly thickened.

To serve, garnish with fried sage leaves and shaved Parmesan cheese.

Serves 4.

Gavi di Gavi
Sauvignon Blanc

Brodo di Pesce/Vegetale*

FISH/VEGETABLE BROTH

2 pounds fish heads, fish strips, prawn shells, or whole fish
2 celery stalks, with leaves, broken into 3 pieces
2 medium carrots, peeled and cut in half
1 large onion, quartered
6 black peppercorns
2 tablespoons salt
3 bay leaves, broken into small pieces
2 tablespoons lobster base (optional)
4 quarts plus 2 cups cold water

Place seafood, celery, carrots, onion, peppercorns, salt, bay leaves, and lobster base in a very large pot. Add cold water and simmer, uncovered, over medium-low heat for 1 hour. Skim surface foam occasionally with a slotted spoon.

Strain broth, discarding solids. Broth can be separated into convenient containers and frozen for later use.

Makes 3 to 4 quarts.

**For vegetable broth, omit fish and lobster base.*

Brodo di Pollo

CHICKEN BROTH

1 chicken, about 4 pounds, cleaned and cut into 6 pieces
2 celery stalks, with leaves, broken into 3 pieces
2 medium carrots, peeled and cut in half
1 large onion, quartered
6 black peppercorns
2 tablespoons salt
3 bay leaves, broken into small pieces
2 tablespoons chicken base (optional)
4 quarts plus 2 cups cold water

Place chicken pieces in a large pot. Add celery, carrots, onion, peppercorns, salt, bay leaves, and chicken base. Pour in cold water and simmer, uncovered, over medium-low heat for 3 hours. Water should barely move. Strain broth, discarding solids. More salt can be added at this point to taste.

The chicken can be served hot or cold with a favorite sauce or in chicken aspic or salad.

To remove fat, in part or completely, let broth cool, then refrigerate for about 2 hours. Fat will solidify on top and can be easily lifted off. Broth can be separated into convenient containers and frozen for later use.

Makes 3 to 4 quarts.

Tè di Zafferano
SAFFRON TEA

1 tablespoon saffron threads
3 cups cold water

Heat a small dry frying pan or skillet to medium low, add saffron threads, and toast lightly, stirring often, for 3 to 5 minutes. Saffron should not turn black. Remove saffron from the pan.

Bring water to a boil in a medium saucepan. Add saffron, reduce heat to low, and simmer for 10 minutes. You can either strain the tea or leave the saffron threads in.

Saffron tea can be stored in a covered container in the refrigerator for up to 1 week or frozen for later use.

Makes 3 cups.

Don't fuss
with the soup.
Soup is not fussy.

4
Pasta

Pasta is a wonderful transition to a hearty meat or fish course. It can also be the highlight of a meal itself, with salad before or after, whatever you feel like.

American ingredients are okay, you can use some American pasta, but it's got to be semolina. Semolina is a special flour ground from durum wheat. The best semolina comes from Italy. It has to be semolina. If you cook with something else, you can call it something else, but don't call it pasta. When you experience the difference, you won't ask me why you can't just use whatever is cheapest at the store. Now, there are some small producers of semolina pasta in the United States. Give them a try; they may be very good.

Don't overcook pasta for nobody. When I serve pasta, it's al dente. When people ask, "Can you cook it longer?" I say, "No." It must have that al dente texture to be Italian pasta. A guy came into the restaurant and wanted his pasta to be cooked longer, and I told him, "It can't be done. Pick something else because it's not right." I didn't charge him for his dinner because there was no way I was going to overcook my pasta.

What people call Italian food in America is not what people cook in Italy. People will say, "I wish you could have pasta with meatballs on your menu." Well, I love meatballs. I make them at home. But you know, it's not a pasta dish. We never had spaghetti and meatballs in Italy. It comes from wanting everything all at once, Pow! There is no staging, no glass of wine, champagne, nothing. You just go, clothes off, done. In Italy, meatballs are the entrée, with fresh peas and marinara. You eat the pasta first, and mama takes it away, and the entrée comes in on a big platter, and it's a beautiful meatball. If I catch you eating the meatball all together with the pasta, I'm gonna poke a fork in you 'cause you're done. Have the pasta first!

Linguine con le Vongole
LINGUINE WITH CLAMS

3 tablespoons extra-virgin olive oil
4 garlic cloves, thinly sliced
1 pound (about 24) Manila clams or New Zealand cockles, scrubbed and rinsed
1/2 cup dry white wine
1 cup canned plum tomatoes, roughly chopped, with juice
Pinch of red pepper flakes
1 pound dried linguine
1/2 cup finely chopped fresh Italian parsley

Heat oil and garlic in a 14- to 16-inch skillet over medium heat until garlic is golden brown. Add clams or cockles, wine, tomatoes, and red pepper flakes. Cover and cook for 7 to 8 minutes, or until the clams have just opened.

Meanwhile, bring 6 quarts of water to a boil in a large pot and add 1/2 tablespoon salt. Drop pasta into the boiling water and cook until almost al dente. Pasta should still be quite firm. Reserve 1 cup of pasta water, then drain linguine into a colander and transfer immediately to the clams.

Cook over high heat for 45 seconds. Stir in parsley. Add some of the reserved pasta water if the linguine seems too dry. Serve in a large bowl.

Serves 4.

Verdicchio
Sauvignon Blanc

Malfatti
SPINACH GNOCCHI

1 1/2 pounds fresh spinach leaves, trimmed, washed, and drained
8 ounces fresh ricotta, drained
1 medium onion, finely chopped
1 egg
1 egg yolk
1 cup freshly grated Parmesan cheese
Salt
Freshly ground black pepper
1 cup all-purpose flour
4 tablespoons unsalted butter
4 fresh sage leaves
Olive oil

Bring a large saucepan of lightly salted water to a boil. Add spinach and cook for 10 seconds. Drain well, squeeze out excess moisture, and finely chop.

In a large mixing bowl, combine spinach, ricotta, onion, egg and extra yolk, 1/2 cup Parmesan, and salt and pepper to taste. Mix very thoroughly with a fork until smooth.

Use a dessert spoon or tablespoon to shape little oval dumplings of the mixture, or roll into small balls between your floured palms, then press to flatten slightly. Coat lightly with flour.

Place butter and sage leaves in a small saucepan and heat gently to melt the butter. Turn off the heat and let stand.

Bring a very large saucepan of lightly salted water to a gentle boil. Add a few drops of olive oil to prevent the dumplings from sticking to one another and then add the dumplings. They should simmer rather than boil. When they bob to the surface, remove with a slotted spoon. Drain well and place in a heated serving dish. Drizzle with the sage-flavored butter. Sprinkle with the remaining grated Parmesan and serve immediately.

Vernaccia
Semillon

Serves 4.

Capellini ai Granchi

CAPELLINI WITH CRAB

2 teaspoons olive oil
3 garlic cloves, diced
1 teaspoon finely chopped fresh rosemary
6 green onions, chopped
4 Roma tomatoes, diced
1 cup dry white wine
1/2 pound snow crab meat
1 cup fish broth (see recipe, page 60)
1/4 cup finely chopped fresh Italian parsley, plus more for garnish
6 fresh basil leaves, chopped
Salt
Freshly ground black pepper
1 pound dried capellini pasta

Heat olive oil in a medium sauté pan over medium heat. Add garlic, rosemary, and onions; cook until garlic is golden. Stir in tomatoes and wine; bring to a boil. Add crab, fish broth, 1/4 cup parsley, basil, and salt and pepper to taste. Reduce heat and simmer for about 6 minutes.

Meanwhile, bring 6 quarts of water to a boil in a large pot and add 1/2 tablespoon salt. Drop pasta into the boiling water and cook until al dente.

Drain pasta and add to the sauce, stirring to coat. Garnish with parsley and serve.

Serves 4.

Gavi di Gavi
Chardonnay

Farfalle all'Uccelletto

FARFALLE WITH CHICKEN, MUSHROOMS, ZUCCHINI, AND TOMATO

1 tablespoon olive oil, plus more for coating pasta
1 pound boneless chicken breasts, cut into 1-inch cubes
1 cup dry white wine
1 pound button mushrooms, sliced lengthwise
3 zucchini, diced
1 onion, diced
Salt
Freshly ground black pepper
1 28-ounce can whole tomatoes, chopped
1 cup water
2 cups heavy cream
1 pound dried farfalle pasta

In a large heavy-bottomed sauté pan, heat 1 tablespoon olive oil until almost smoking. Add chicken and cook on high for 2 minutes. Pour in wine and cook until reduced slightly. Add mushrooms, zucchini, onion, and salt and pepper to taste; cook on medium heat for 15 minutes. Reduce heat, add tomatoes, and simmer for 5 minutes. Add water, then slowly stir in cream.

Meanwhile, bring 6 quarts of water to a boil in a large pot and add 1/2 tablespoon salt. Drop pasta into the boiling water and cook until al dente. Drain and toss with a little oil.

Transfer pasta to a large serving bowl, add sauce, and toss. Serve with thick-crusted Tuscan bread.

Valpolicella
Syrah

Serves 6.

About six or seven years ago I discovered that the Three Tenors would be singing in a small theater in Vancouver, B.C. I tried to get tickets, but the concert was sold out, so I said to my wife, "We are going to go anyway." I drove over to the ticket place and said, "I'm Mauro Golmarvi and I have will-call tickets." They said, "There is no will-call for you, although we do have two tickets that nobody claimed." We were so excited. We went to our hotel room, changed, and then went to a place to eat. They had this dish that included prawns, tomatoes, and cream, and it sounded so good. I ordered it and it was not good. I knew that I could go back and make this dish right. Well, it became the number one selling pasta in our restaurant because I knew how to balance the flavors. I used fresh ingredients, and I don't overcook pasta for nobody.

Linguine alla Mauro

LINGUINE WITH EGGPLANT, TOMATO, PRAWNS, AND CREAM

2 tablespoons olive oil
1 tablespoon chopped garlic
1 eggplant, cut into 1/2-inch cubes
2 cups marinara (see recipe, page 81)
1 cup dry white wine
1/2 teaspoon salt
1/2 teaspoon freshly ground black pepper
1 1/2 pounds fresh jumbo prawns, about 16 to 20
1/2 cup heavy cream
1 pound dried linguine
6 fresh basil leaves, chopped
8 sprigs fresh Italian parsley, finely chopped

Heat olive oil in a large sauté pan over medium heat. Add garlic and eggplant and sauté until garlic is golden. Stir in marinara and wine; bring to a boil. Stir in salt, pepper, prawns, and cream. Reduce to a simmer and cook for about 6 minutes.

Meanwhile, bring 6 quarts of water to a boil in a large pot and add 1/2 tablespoon salt. Drop pasta into the boiling water and cook until al dente.

Drain pasta and add to the sauce with the basil, stirring to coat. Garnish with parsley and serve.

Serves 4.

Morellino
Merlot

Fettuccine ai Gamberetti

FETTUCCINE WITH SHRIMP

6 tablespoons extra-virgin olive oil
1 tablespoon unsalted butter
3 garlic cloves, thinly sliced
1/2 teaspoon salt
1/2 teaspoon freshly ground black pepper
1 pound rock shrimp or medium shrimp, peeled
1 medium zucchini, cut into 1/4-inch-thick half-moons (about 1 cup)
1/2 teaspoon red pepper flakes
1 cup dry white wine
2 Roma tomatoes, diced
1/2 teaspoon chopped fresh basil
Juice of 1/2 lemon
1 pound dried fettuccine pasta
1 tablespoon finely chopped fresh Italian parsley

In a 12- to 14-inch sauté pan, heat 4 tablespoons olive oil, butter, garlic, salt, and pepper over medium heat and cook until garlic is light golden brown, about 2 to 3 minutes. Add shrimp and cook until red on both sides, about 2 minutes. Add zucchini pieces and cook until just soft, about 2 to 3 minutes. Add red pepper flakes, wine, tomatoes, basil, and lemon juice; bring to a boil and cook for 2 minutes.

Meanwhile, bring 6 quarts of water to a boil in a large pot and add 1/2 tablespoon salt. Drop pasta into the boiling water and cook until al dente.

Drain pasta and toss into the sauce. Remove from the heat and toss with parsley and remaining 2 tablespoons olive oil. Pour into a heated bowl and serve with plenty of pepper.

Chardonnay
Sauvignon Blanc

Serves 4.

Fettuccine al Sugo di Carne

FETTUCCINE WITH MEAT SAUCE

4 tablespoons olive oil
2 garlic cloves, minced
1 pound beef sirloin, cut into 1/2-inch strips or ground
1 pound crimini mushrooms, sliced
1/2 cup red table wine
2 cups marinara (see recipe, page 81)
1/2 teaspoon salt
1/2 teaspoon freshly ground black pepper
1/2 cup veal or beef broth (see recipe, page 57)
1 pound dried fettuccine pasta
1/4 cup freshly grated Parmesan cheese
2 fresh basil leaves, thinly sliced

Heat 3 tablespoons olive oil in a medium saucepan over medium-high heat. Add garlic and cook, stirring occasionally, until it turns pale gold. Add beef strips and stir several times to brown on all sides. Add mushrooms and sauté for 2 minutes. Add wine and simmer for 2 minutes more. Add marinara, salt, pepper, and broth and turn ingredients over 2 or 3 times. Cook at a steady but gentle simmer for 5 minutes.

Meanwhile, bring 6 quarts of water to a boil in a large pot and add 1/2 tablespoon salt. Drop pasta into the boiling water and cook until al dente.

Drain pasta and toss immediately and thoroughly with the sauce. Sprinkle with Parmesan, remaining olive oil, and basil, then serve.

Serves 4.

Rosso Conero
Zinfandel

Don't overcook pasta for nobody.

Fusilli Veneziana

FUSILLI WITH BEEF, SPINACH, AND TOMATO SAUCE

1 pound lean ground beef
1 medium onion, finely chopped
8 ounces fresh spinach
1 cup red table wine
2 cups canned Italian tomatoes, coarsely chopped
Salt
Freshly ground black pepper
1 pound dried fusilli pasta
1 cup freshly grated Parmesan cheese

In a large sauté pan, cook ground beef over medium heat until browned; drain. Add onion and spinach; cook for 1 minute. Add wine and cook, stirring, for 4 minutes. Add tomatoes, reduce heat, and simmer for 10 minutes. Season to taste with salt and pepper.

Meanwhile, bring 6 quarts of water to a boil in a large pot and add 1/2 tablespoon salt. Drop pasta into the boiling water and cook until al dente.

Drain pasta and add to the sauce, stirring to thoroughly coat. Garnish with Parmesan and serve.

Serves 4.

Lagrein
Meritage

This recipe was featured in Bon Appétit *magazine, May 1997, Special Collector's Edition.*

Fusilli Zafferano

FUSILLI WITH SAFFRON

One day I saw an Italian opera singer sitting at my corner table, so I had to think of something we could cook that was special. I walked into the cooler. We had lots of pork, whole suckling pigs. We had pine nuts, spinach. We had a machine to grind our own sausage. But what pasta to use? I couldn't imagine that this would go with spaghetti because it would fall off. I needed a pasta that could hold the sauce. It would fall off penne because it is a loose sauce. So I thought of fusilli because it has that rotation going on and has body. So when you put a spoon in it, I guarantee that in each spoonful you will get currants, pine nuts, saffron, and a little sausage. It's not a fork dish, it's a spoon dish.

1 pound dried fusilli pasta
2 tablespoons olive oil, plus more for coating pasta
12 ounces spicy Italian bulk sausage or links with casings removed
2 tablespoons pine nuts
2 tablespoons Zante currants
1 ounce saffron tea (see recipe, page 62)
1 cup heavy cream
1/2 teaspoon salt
1/2 teaspoon freshly ground black pepper
2 cups arugula
1/3 cup grated Pecorino Romano cheese

Cook pasta in a large pot of lightly salted boiling water until al dente. Drain, toss with a little olive oil, and set aside.

In a large sauté pan, heat 2 tablespoons olive oil over medium heat until almost smoking. Add sausage, breaking it up into small pieces, and brown evenly. When sausage is cooked, add pine nuts and sauté for 1 minute. Add currants and saffron tea, stirring to deglaze the pan. Add cream, salt, and pepper and reduce until fairly thick, but not too thick! Add arugula, 1/4 cup grated cheese, and pasta. Stir until thoroughly combined and arugula is just wilted. Garnish with remaining cheese and serve.

Serves 4.

Gattinara
Pinot Noir

Rigatoni alla Pepperonata e Salsiccia
RIGATONI WITH PEPPERS AND SAUSAGE

2 tablespoons extra-virgin olive oil
4 mild Italian link sausages, sliced
2 red bell peppers, roasted and sliced
1 garlic clove, minced
1/4 cup red table wine
2 cups marinara
3/4 cup heavy cream
6 fresh basil leaves, torn
1 pound dried rigatoni pasta
Freshly shaved Parmesan cheese

Heat oil in a large saucepan over medium heat. Add sausage, peppers, and garlic. When sausage is partially cooked, add wine and continue cooking until reduced, about 6 minutes. Stir in marinara and cream and cook to reduce by half. Add basil.

Meanwhile, bring 6 quarts of water to a boil in a large pot and add 1/2 tablespoon salt. Drop pasta into the boiling water and cook until al dente.

Drain pasta and mix with the sauce. Sprinkle with shaved Parmesan.

Serves 4.

Montepulciano
Cabernet Sauvignon

Marinara
TOMATO SAUCE

2 tablespoons olive oil
3/4 cup chopped onion
2 garlic cloves, chopped
1 cup dry white wine
2 28-ounce cans whole peeled plum tomatoes
1 carrot, peeled and quartered lengthwise
1 celery stalk, halved lengthwise
1/2 teaspoon salt
1/2 teaspoon freshly ground black pepper
6 fresh basil leaves

Heat olive oil in a medium sauté pan over medium heat. Add onion and sauté until translucent. (For a slightly sweeter sauce, sauté until onion begins to caramelize.) Add garlic and sauté until it begins to brown. Add wine and simmer over medium heat until the alcohol cooks off and the liquid is reduced by half, about 5 minutes. Pour in tomatoes and mash with a whisk or spoon; bring to a boil.

Bundle carrot and celery sticks and tie with kitchen string, then add to the sauce. Stir in salt and pepper, reduce heat to low, and simmer at least 30 minutes, or until the tomatoes break up and the mixture is smooth. Add basil leaves for the last 10 minutes of cooking. Remove carrot and celery before serving.

Makes 6 cups.

Pappardelle Bolognese

PAPPARDELLE WITH MEAT SAUCE

1/3 cup olive oil
1 1/2 medium onions, minced
2 celery stalks, finely chopped
2 large carrots, peeled and finely chopped
1/2 pound lean ground beef
1/2 pound lean ground pork
1/2 pound mild Italian bulk sausage or links with casings removed
1/2 cup red table wine
2 28-ounce cans peeled Italian tomatoes with juice, pureed
1 1/2 cups beef broth (see recipe, page 57) plus 1 1/2 cups water,
or 3 cups water
1/2 teaspoon salt
1/2 teaspoon freshly ground black pepper
1/4 teaspoon grated nutmeg
2 pounds fresh or dried pappardelle pasta
2 tablespoons chopped fresh Italian parsley
1/3 cup grated Parmesan cheese

Heat olive oil in a large high-sided saucepan over medium heat. Add onions, celery, and carrots; sauté until vegetables are limp and onions are translucent. Add ground meat and cook, stirring often to break up meat, until no longer pink.

Turn heat to high, add wine, and cook until alcohol evaporates, about 1 to 2 minutes. Add pureed tomatoes and stir to mix well. Add broth and/or water and bring to a gentle simmer. Add salt, pepper, and nutmeg. Cook, uncovered, over medium-low heat for about 2 hours, stirring frequently. The liquid will reduce; if the sauce becomes dry, add a bit more water.

Meanwhile, bring 6 quarts of water to a boil in a large pot and add 1/2 tablespoon salt. Drop pasta into the boiling water and cook until al dente.

Quickly drain pasta and place in a serving bowl. Add meat sauce, parsley, and grated Parmesan. Toss pasta and sauce, and serve immediately.

Serves 4 to 6.

Rosso di Montalcino
Cabernet Sauvignon

Ravioli Cappesante
RAVIOLI WITH SCALLOPS

2 tablespoons unsalted butter
1 pound fresh sea scallops
1/2 cup dry white wine
2 tablespoons saffron tea (see recipe, page 62)
1 cup heavy cream
6 green onions, coarsely chopped
Salt
Freshly ground black pepper
1 pound fresh cheese ravioli
2 tablespoons finely chopped fresh Italian parsley

Melt butter in a large sauté pan over medium-high heat. Add scallops and sear on both sides. Add wine and cook until wine evaporates. Add saffron tea and cream; reduce heat to medium-low and cook for about 6 minutes. Add green onions and cook for about 3 minutes. Season to taste with salt and pepper.

Meanwhile, bring 6 quarts of water to a boil in a large pot and add 1/2 tablespoon salt. Drop ravioli into the boiling water and cook until al dente.

Drain ravioli, add to the sauce, and stir to coat. Garnish with parsley and serve.

Pinot Grigio
Pinot Gris

Serves 4.

Ricotta, pecorino, and Parmesan are good cheeses for ravioli.

Penne alla Vodka

PENNE WITH VODKA, PANCETTA, TOMATO, AND CREAM SAUCE

2 teaspoons unsalted butter
1 cup chopped pancetta
10 pink peppercorns
6 green onions, coarsely chopped
6 fresh basil leaves, chopped
6 sprigs fresh Italian parsley, finely chopped
2 teaspoons vodka
1 pint heavy cream
5 ounces marinara (see recipe, page 81)
Salt
Freshly ground black pepper
1 pound dried penne pasta

Melt butter in a large sauté pan over medium heat. Add pancetta, peppercorns, onions, basil, and parsley; cook until butter is golden. Add vodka and continue to cook for 30 seconds. Reduce heat, add cream and marinara, and simmer for 8 minutes, or until cream and marinara marry. Season to taste with salt and pepper.

Meanwhile, bring 6 quarts of water to a boil in a large pot and add 1/2 tablespoon salt. Drop pasta into the boiling water and cook until al dente.

Drain pasta and add to the sauce. Stir and serve.

Super Tuscan
Meritage

Serves 4.

Ravioli Maruzza
RAVIOLI WITH WILD MUSHROOMS

1 tablespoon unsalted butter
2 cups sliced wild mushrooms
1/4 cup chopped green onions
Salt
Freshly ground black pepper
1/4 cup red table wine
1/4 cup sweet Marsala
1/4 cup demi-glace
1/2 cup heavy cream
32 pieces large cheese ravioli, frozen or fresh

Combine butter, mushrooms, green onions, and salt and pepper to taste in a large sauté pan. Cook over high heat for 3 to 5 minutes. Add red wine, Marsala, demi-glace, and cream. Continue cooking until the sauce thickens.

Meanwhile, bring 6 quarts of water to a boil in a large pot and add 1/2 tablespoon salt. Drop ravioli into the boiling water and cook until al dente.

Drain ravioli and add to the sauce, stirring to thoroughly coat.

Serves 4.

Barbera
Syrah

Spaghetti con Funghi
SPAGHETTI WITH PORCINI MUSHROOMS

14 ounces porcini mushrooms, trimmed
1 cup veal broth (see recipe, page 57)
3 tablespoons fine olive oil
3/4 cup finely chopped onion
1 garlic clove, finely chopped
2 ounces prosciutto, cut into thin strips
7 ounces tomatoes, peeled, seeded, and diced
Salt
Freshly ground white pepper
1 pound dried spaghetti
2 tablespoons chopped fresh Italian parsley
Freshly shaved Parmesan cheese

Slice porcini lengthwise, keeping the original shape when possible.

Bring veal broth to a boil in a saucepan and cook until it is reduced to one-third of its original volume.

Heat olive oil in a medium skillet over low heat. Add onion and garlic, cover, and cook gently until lightly colored. Add prosciutto and sauté briefly. Add mushrooms, tomatoes, and salt and pepper to taste; cover and simmer for 4 to 5 minutes. Pour in reduced veal broth and simmer, uncovered, over medium heat for 20 minutes, or until the liquid has almost completely evaporated.

Meanwhile, bring 6 quarts of water to a boil in a large pot and add 1/2 tablespoon salt. Drop pasta into the boiling water and cook until al dente.

Drain pasta and add to the sauce with the parsley, stirring to coat. Heat until piping hot. Serve with freshly shaved Parmesan.

Barolo
Cabernet Franc

Serves 4.

5
Risotto

Risotto is Italian rice that has been coated and toasted lightly in butter or olive oil and onion (called the *soffrito*) and then cooked by gradually adding small amounts of broth while stirring. This allows the rice to release its starch and makes the dish thick and creamy.

It takes passion to stir and cook the risotto till it's perfect. It's good that it takes a little time. You taste that time and effort in every bite. That's what makes it good for the soul, both making and eating it.

I like to make risotto with short-grained Italian Arborio rice because it produces a creaminess that is unique. You can also use Carnaroli or Vialone Nano.

I said this about pasta and now I'm saying it about risotto: don't overcook it for nobody. It's gotta be al dente. When is it al dente? Put a piece of dried rice or pasta in your mouth and give it a chew or two. Al dente is when it loses that crunch, but just when it loses that crunch. This is *not* soggy-noodle-sticky-rice. This means you should taste your risotto often while you are stirring it so that you can pull it off the flame and serve it just when the moisture has made it through the grain of rice. When you are thinking, "It might be done but I'm not sure," then it's done. Take it off the stove and get it on the plate to eat. If you wait until you are thinking, "It's done," it's probably overdone.

The basic risotto recipe is the foundation from which you can prepare all kinds of wonderful risotto dishes. And on its own, with a little Parmigiano-Reggiano, it is a perfect, simple accompaniment for meat and vegetable dishes.

Risotto

3 tablespoons unsalted butter
1/2 cup diced onion
1 cup Arborio rice
1/2 cup dry white wine
1 cup water
1/2 cup chicken, beef, or fish broth (see recipes, pages 61, 57, and 60)
1/2 teaspoon salt
1/2 teaspoon freshly ground black pepper

Melt 1 1/2 tablespoons butter in a heavy-bottomed sauté pan over low heat. Add onion and sauté until translucent. Add rice and cook, stirring constantly, for 3 to 4 minutes. Add wine and 1/2 cup water. Cook, stirring constantly, until all liquid is absorbed. Add remaining water and cook, stirring constantly, until absorbed. Add broth, salt, pepper, and remaining butter. Simmer until the rice is just cooked and has a creamy texture.

Serves 2 (4 as a side dish).

Risotto al Tartufo Bianco

RISOTTO WITH WHITE TRUFFLE

6 cups vegetable broth (see recipe, page 60)
6 tablespoons butter
1/2 cup finely chopped onion
3 cups Arborio rice
1/2 teaspoon salt
1/2 teaspoon freshly ground black pepper
4 ounces freshly grated Parmesan cheese
2 whole white truffles

In a large pot, bring vegetable broth to a boil. Reduce heat to low, and simmer.

Melt 4 tablespoons butter in a large heavy-bottomed sauté pan over low heat. Add onion and sauté until translucent. Add rice, salt, and pepper and cook, stirring constantly, for 3 to 4 minutes. Gradually add hot broth, 1 cup at a time, stirring constantly, ensuring that the liquid is fully absorbed by the rice before adding more. Continue stirring and adding stock until the rice is just cooked and has a creamy texture, about 15 minutes. Stir in remaining 2 tablespoons butter.

Remove risotto to a serving dish. Sprinkle with Parmesan. Then, using a truffle shaver, shave paper-thin slices of white truffle over the finished risotto. Serve immediately.

Serves 6.

Chianti
Cabernet Franc

Risotto alla Boscaiola

RISOTTO WITH WILD MUSHROOMS AND PANCETTA

6 tablespoons unsalted butter
2 ounces dried porcini mushrooms,
 soaked in warm water for 30 minutes and drained
6 ounces fresh wild mushrooms
 (shiitake, oyster, and porcini)
4 ounces pancetta or prosciutto, cut in 1/4-inch cubes
1/2 cup red table wine
1/2 cup Sicilian Marsala
1/3 cup chicken broth (see recipe, page 61)
3 green onions, chopped
1/2 teaspoon salt
1/2 teaspoon freshly ground black pepper
1/3 cup heavy cream
4 to 5 cups veal or chicken broth (see recipes,
 pages 57 and 61)
1/2 cup diced white onion
2 cups Arborio rice
3/4 cup dry white wine
1/2 cup freshly grated Parmesan cheese
1 tablespoon chopped fresh Italian parsley

Melt 4 tablespoons butter in a medium saucepan over medium heat. Add mushrooms and pancetta and cook for about 3 minutes. Stir in red wine, Marsala, 1/3 cup chicken broth, green onions, salt, and pepper; cook for 3 minutes. Add cream, reduce heat to low, and cook until thickened, about 8 minutes. Set aside.

Meanwhile, place 4 to 5 cups veal or chicken broth in a large pot and bring to a boil. Reduce heat to low and keep at a simmer.

Melt remaining 2 tablespoons butter in an 8-quart saucepan over low heat. Add white onion and cook until translucent, stirring occasionally, about 3 minutes. Increase heat to medium, quickly add rice, and cook, stirring constantly, until the grains start to become translucent, 3 to 4 minutes. Pour in white wine and continue stirring until most of the liquid is absorbed, about 2 minutes. Gradually add hot broth, 1/2 cup at a time, stirring constantly, ensuring that the liquid is fully absorbed by the rice before adding more. Continue stirring and adding stock for 12 minutes.

Pour the mushroom-cream sauce into the rice mixture and continue to stir and simmer until the rice is just cooked and has a creamy texture, about 2 to 3 minutes. Stir in Parmesan and sprinkle with parsley. Serve immediately.

Barbera
Syrah

Serves 4 to 6.

Risotto al Pomodoro e Carne

RISOTTO WITH TOMATO AND FILET MIGNON

1 14-ounce can whole tomatoes
2 tablespoons olive oil
1 tablespoon unsalted butter
2 garlic cloves, minced
1 onion, chopped
12 ounces filet mignon, thinly sliced
2 cups Arborio rice
3/4 cup red table wine
1 1/2 cups veal broth, warmed (see recipe, page 57)
1/4 teaspoon salt
1/4 teaspoon freshly ground black pepper
1/2 cup water
1/2 cup freshly grated Parmigiano-Reggiano cheese
1 tablespoon chopped fresh Italian parsley
1 tablespoon chopped fresh basil

Be sure to buy high-quality canned tomatoes for your recipes. I like the Italian brand San Marzano. It always tastes better when you mash the whole canned tomatoes with your hand rather than just using canned crushed tomatoes.

Pour canned tomatoes into a bowl and smash by hand until the tomatoes are mostly broken up into pieces. Set aside.

Heat olive oil and butter in a large sauté pan over high heat. Add garlic and allow butter to brown. Add onion and stir for about 3 minutes. Add beef, reduce heat to simmer, and cook until the meat turns white, about 3 minutes.

Stir in rice, increase heat to medium, and cook, stirring constantly, until rice turns brown. Add wine and stir until liquid is absorbed. Add veal broth, 1/2 cup at a time, and cook, stirring constantly, until the liquid is completely absorbed before adding more. This process should take about 10 minutes.

Add smashed tomatoes and continue stirring. Season with salt and pepper as moisture is being absorbed. Stir in water. Once water is absorbed and the risotto is almost finished (about 18 minutes from when the rice was added), stir in cheese, reserving 1 tablespoon for garnish. Continue stirring for about 2 minutes, or until the rice is just cooked and has a creamy texture, then turn off heat.

Let risotto sit for about 3 minutes, uncovered, then transfer to a serving bowl. Garnish with remaining cheese, parsley, and basil.

Serves 4.

Aglianico
Merlot

It always tastes better when you mash the whole canned tomatoes with your hand rather than just using canned crushed tomatoes.

Risotto ai Frutti di Mare
SEAFOOD RISOTTO

1 1/2 pounds monkfish
1 pound clams
1 pound mussels
5 1/2 cups water or fish broth (see recipe, page 60)
2 carrots, peeled and cut into 1/2-inch pieces
2 celery stalks, trimmed and cut into 1/2-inch pieces
1 bay leaf
5 white peppercorns
3/4 teaspoon salt, divided
3 tablespoons butter
8 scallops*
1 pound shrimp, peeled and deveined
1/2 cup finely chopped onion
1 garlic clove, finely chopped
1 1/2 cups Arborio rice
1/4 teaspoon freshly ground black pepper
1/2 cup white wine
1 tablespoon chopped fresh Italian parsley

Bone monkfish and slice into 3/4-inch pieces. Wash and scrub clams and mussels well under cold running water, discarding any open clams and mussels. Remove the beard from the mussels.

Place water, carrots, celery, bay leaf, peppercorns, and 1/2 teaspoon salt in a large pot (if fish broth is used, vegetables and seasonings are not necessary). Bring to a boil, then reduce heat. Add monkfish and simmer for 5 minutes. Lift out fish and set aside.

Bring the liquid back to a boil. Add clams and mussels, and cook until the shells open. Lift out shellfish, discarding any that remain closed. Strain the broth and reserve 3 cups.

Melt butter in a large casserole over medium heat. Add scallops and sauté for 1 minute on each side. Lift out and set aside. Add shrimp and sauté for 2 minutes. Lift out and set aside with scallops.

Reduce heat to medium-low, add onion and garlic to the casserole, and sauté until onion is translucent. Add rice, 1/4 teaspoon salt, and pepper, and cook, stirring constantly, for 3 to 4 minutes. Add wine and cook, stirring constantly, for 3 minutes, or until it is absorbed. Gradually add reserved broth, 1/2 cup at a time, stirring constantly, and ensuring that the liquid is fully absorbed by the rice before adding more. Continue stirring and adding broth until the rice is just cooked and has a creamy texture, about 15 minutes.

Shuck clams and mussels, leaving a few in their shells. Mix fish, shucked clams and mussels, scallops, and shrimp into the risotto in the last few minutes of cooking to warm them through. Adjust seasoning if necessary, then sprinkle with parsley, garnish the risotto with reserved clams and mussels in their shells, and serve immediately from the casserole.

Pinot Grigio
Sauvignon Blanc

Serves 4 to 6.

* *When they're in season, you can use whole singing scallops in this dish for added color and flavor. Buy small scallops and cook them as you would the clams and mussels.*

Risotto Sienese

RISOTTO WITH PROSCIUTTO, PEAS, AND GORGONZOLA

1 1/2 tablespoons butter
4 ounces prosciutto, cut into thin strips
1/4 teaspoon salt
1/4 teaspoon freshly ground black pepper
1/2 cup dry white wine
3 cups chicken broth (see recipe, page 61)
2 cups heavy cream
1/2 cup (2 to 3 ounces) crumbled Gorgonzola cheese
2 cups Arborio rice
1 cup peas (fresh or frozen)
1/4 to 1/2 cup freshly grated Parmesan cheese

Melt butter in a large heavy-bottomed sauté pan over medium heat. Add prosciutto, salt, and pepper; sauté for 2 minutes. Add wine, chicken broth, and cream. Turn heat to medium-high and bring to a boil, stirring (about 5 minutes). Add Gorgonzola and stir to melt in.

Add rice and reduce heat to medium-low. Cook for 15 minutes, stirring often. Add peas and continue to stir until liquid is mostly cooked out and rice is just cooked and has a creamy texture (about 3 minutes). Stir in Parmesan and serve immediately.

Serves 4 to 6.

Vino Nobile di Montepulciano
Syrah

Risotto con Oregonzola
RISOTTO WITH BLUE CHEESE

2 tablespoons olive oil, plus more for garnish
1 tablespoon unsalted butter
1 medium yellow or white onion, diced
2 cups Arborio rice
1/8 teaspoon saffron threads (about 7 threads) or 1/2 cup saffron tea
(see recipe, page 62)
3 cups chicken broth, warmed (see recipe, page 61)
1/2 cup dry white wine
1 cup heavy cream
5 ounces Oregonzola blue cheese (or Gorgonzola), plus more for garnish
3 tablespoons chopped fresh chives
1 tablespoon freshly grated Parmigiano-Reggiano cheese

Heat 2 tablespoons olive oil and butter in a large sauté pan over high heat. When butter turns brown, add onion and cook, stirring, until translucent. Add rice and cook, stirring constantly, until rice is translucent, about 4 minutes. Add saffron. Reduce heat to medium and add chicken broth, 1/2 cup at a time, stirring constantly, ensuring that the liquid is fully absorbed by the rice before adding more. This process should take about 12 minutes. Add wine and continue to stir for about 2 minutes. Add cream and stir for another 2 minutes.

Crumble 5 ounces Oregonzola into the risotto and stir for about 2 minutes. Stir in 2 tablespoons chives and cook for another 2 minutes, or until the rice is just cooked and has a creamy texture.

Transfer risotto to serving plates. Garnish with remaining chives, a few crumbles of Oregonzola, a drizzle of olive oil, and a sprinkle of Parmigiano-Reggiano.

Serves 4.

Valpolicella "Ripassa"
Cabernet Sauvignon

6
Piatto Forte

Iram and I do all the shopping for Assaggio. Some call their broker about the stock market; I call the fish market when I'm having my coffee in the morning. I let what is fresh determine the menu at the restaurant. I never ask the price, but I insist on knowing if it's fresh today. You should do the same. Smell everything when you buy it, especially shellfish. It should smell like the ocean, but not fishy. It's important to develop a good relationship with the person who sells you your fish. Buy from the same person year after year, and you will get to know and trust each other. I've never had a bad fish from my fish guy. Even when other people have offered me a cheaper price, I won't take it. Why mess up that relationship? This is the guy who makes sure you get the best. He's like family — he should be at your son's birthday party, your daughter's graduation. Treat him like your brother; he is your stomach's best friend.

High-quality fresh ingredients are the most important part of cooking. When I say veal chop, I mean a milk-fed veal chop. It is worth it to get the best. The same goes for rack of lamb, fish, ravioli, scallops, everything. If you can't find good quality, then change your ingredients rather than settle for mediocre. If the scallops don't look good, use prawns or lobster tail. You are being adaptive but keeping it fresh. If Mauro says to use halibut, but you can't find good halibut, and cod is in season, use the cod. It's okay.

Salmon is a special gift of the region. I don't even have to tell you that it has to be wild salmon. You know it. This fish has a wonderful high fat content and should not be dressed up with lots of spices and flavors. It drives me crazy when people overpower the salmon. Someone will say, "I had this beautiful salmon with melted cheese on it." Excuse me? In Italy we say you can't combine ocean and mountain (*mare e montagna*). So don't use Parmesan on your fish. The fish swims and the cow walks — you can't blend these two. Never. Well, I might understand if you are using a light goat cheese or something very light, it's okay. But sharp cheese with fish? It just can't be done. It's against the laws of nature! You must be a food criminal!

Porchetta con Portobello

STUFFED PORK CHOPS WITH PORTOBELLO MUSHROOMS AND RISOTTO

4 pork loin chops, 2 1/2 to 3 inches thick*
4 thin slices prosciutto
4 thin slices fontina cheese
8 fresh sage leaves
Olive oil
Salt
Freshly ground black pepper

Sauce:
2 tablespoons olive oil
2 garlic cloves, coarsely chopped
Salt
Freshly ground black pepper
2 medium portobello mushrooms, stemmed and cut into 1/4-inch slices
3/8 cup Barolo wine
1 cup veal broth (see recipe, page 57)
2 tablespoons unsalted butter
1 tablespoon flour

Risotto:
2 tablespoons unsalted butter
1/2 cup diced (1/4-inch) onion
1 cup Arborio rice
1/2 cup Barolo wine
1 cup water, at a rolling boil
1/2 cup hot veal broth (see recipe, page 57)
Salt
Freshly ground black pepper

Prepare a gas or charcoal grill for medium heat.

Lay each pork or veal chop flat on a cutting board. Make an opening in the side of the chop to the bone. Carefully hollow out the inside to about 1/4 inch from the edges, being careful not to pierce the sides. For each chop, stack 1 slice of prosciutto, 1 slice of fontina, and 2 sage leaves, and fold over once. Stuff the chops, spreading the stuffing evenly. Brush with olive oil and season with salt and pepper to taste. Place on a plate, set aside, and prepare the sauce.

To prepare the sauce, heat olive oil in a heavy-bottomed sauté pan over medium heat. Add garlic and salt and pepper to taste; cook until garlic is golden brown. Add mushrooms and sauté for 1 minute. Stir in wine and cook to reduce by half. Add veal broth and cook to reduce by two-thirds.

In a small sauté pan, melt 2 tablespoons butter over low heat. Add 1 tablespoon flour and cook, whisking, for 2 minutes. Stir into the sauce and cook until the sauce is fairly thick and shiny. Set aside, keep warm, and prepare the risotto.

To prepare the risotto, melt 1 1/2 tablespoons butter in a heavy-bottomed sauté pan over low heat. Add onion and sauté until translucent. Add rice and cook, stirring constantly, for 3 to 4 minutes. Add wine and 1/2 cup water. Cook, stirring constantly, until all liquid is absorbed. Add remaining water and cook, stirring constantly, until absorbed. Add hot veal broth, salt and pepper to taste, and remaining butter. Simmer until the rice is just cooked and has a creamy texture.

Grill the stuffed chops until just cooked through, about 4 to 6 minutes per side. Cooking time will vary according to the size of the chops. When the chops are nearly finished grilling, place some risotto in the center of each plate. Place a chop on the mound of risotto with the bone side facing in. Divide the sauce equally among the plates. If the sauce has become too dry, add water or veal broth.

Serves 4. *Brunello*
Cabernet Sauvignon

**This recipe can also be made with veal chops.*

Agnello Marchigiana

BRAISED LAMB SHANKS

4 lamb hind shanks
1 cup red table wine
1 cup veal or beef broth (see recipe, page 57)
1 cup tomato sauce
1 28-ounce can plum tomatoes, crushed
3 bay leaves
1 sprig fresh rosemary, chopped
1/4 teaspoon ground cinnamon
2 tablespoons thinly sliced fresh basil
2 small onions, quartered and sliced into 1/4-inch half-circles
1/2 teaspoon salt
1/2 teaspoon freshly ground black pepper

Preheat oven to 350°F.

Trim lamb shanks and place in a medium roasting pan or casserole. Combine remaining ingredients in a bowl; pour over the lamb shanks. Cover with foil and braise in the oven, turning occasionally, for 4 to 5 hours, or until tender.

Serves 4.

Amarone
Zinfandel

Vitello al Limone (Piccata*)
VEAL WITH LEMON SAUCE

1/2 cup flour
1/2 teaspoon salt
1/2 teaspoon freshly ground black pepper
14 ounces veal round, cut into 4 slices
2 tablespoons olive oil
1 lemon
1/2 cup dry white wine
1/2 cup veal broth (see recipe, page 57)
2 tablespoons chopped fresh Italian parsley
1 tablespoon unsalted butter

Mix flour, salt, and pepper on a large plate. Lay a piece of plastic wrap on a cutting board. Place 1 veal slice on top and cover with another piece of plastic wrap. Pound veal flat with a meat tenderizer or mallet, starting at the center and working out to the edges. Each slice of veal should be 8 to 10 inches across and less than 1/4 inch thick.

Heat olive oil in a large sauté pan over high heat. Dredge veal slices in flour mixture and place in the pan. Cook for 1 1/2 minutes per side. If all 4 slices will not fit in one layer in the pan, cook 2 slices at a time, returning all 4 to the pan when cooked. Squeeze in juice of lemon and add wine, veal broth, and 1 tablespoon parsley. Stir and cook for 3 minutes. Transfer veal to a large serving platter.

Add butter to the pan, stir, and reduce sauce over high heat, about 2 minutes. Pour sauce over veal. Garnish with remaining parsley and serve immediately.

Serves 4.

Pinot Grigio
Pinot Gris

**For Vitello Piccata, add 1 tablespoon drained capers as the sauce is reducing.*

Ossobuco alla Milanese

BRAISED VEAL SHANKS

4 slices veal shank, each 2 inches thick, tied with kitchen string
1/2 teaspoon salt
1/2 teaspoon freshly ground black pepper
1/2 cup all-purpose flour
2 tablespoons unsalted butter
4 tablespoons olive oil
1 small yellow onion, finely chopped
2 carrots, peeled and diced
2 stalks celery, diced
1/2 teaspoon grated lemon zest
1 heaping tablespoon capers
2 anchovy fillets in olive oil
1/4 cup chopped fresh Italian parsley
1 cup red table wine
2 cups meat broth (see recipe, page 57)
1 28-ounce can tomatoes, peeled, quartered, seeded, and smashed

Preheat oven to 350°F. Carefully wash veal under cold running water and pat dry with paper towels. Season with salt and pepper. Dredge in flour, tapping off any excess.

Melt butter and olive oil in a large flameproof casserole (10 by 12 by 4 inches) over gentle heat. Brown veal slices on both sides, about 5 minutes per side. Remove veal and set aside. Increase heat to medium, add onion, and sauté for 2 minutes. Reduce heat to low and add carrots and celery; cover and cook until vegetables are tender, about 7 minutes.

Meanwhile, puree lemon zest, capers, and anchovies in a food processor. A little olive oil can be added to make it smooth.

Return veal to the casserole. Sprinkle with anchovy puree and parsley. Add wine, meat broth, and tomatoes; simmer, uncovered, for 5 minutes. Liquid should come just to the top of the veal shanks. Add more broth if necessary. Cover with foil and braise in the oven for 1 1/2 to 2 hours, basting veal with sauce and turning occasionally, until it is tender.

Serve with risotto (see recipe, page 92).

Serves 4.

Barolo
Meritage

Cooking at the James Beard House, December 27, 2004.

It was such an honor to be invited to cook at the famous James Beard House that I had the whole thing planned out way ahead of time. We had the ingredients lined up to make dinner for 100 people: meat, fish, pasta, everything. That's when it all started going crazy. We sent the crab overnight, but it got there just after the James Beard House closed on Thursday afternoon. It went back to the FedEx office and it began to smell. It spoiled. No way was I going to use it now, so I carried fresh crab packed in ice with me on the airplane to New York. I didn't even want it in the cargo hold.

When we arrived, we started working on our tiramisu, but the kitchen didn't have enough refrigerator space for the sheet pans. It was snowing and freezing cold outside, though, so we had the tiramisu stacked up right outside the door.

We had ordered polenta as part of the antipasto, but the polenta we received was soft rather than hard. The idea was to grill squares of the hard polenta and serve with 20-year-old balsamic and a special wine from the Pacific Northwest. So the wine was there, the balsamic was there, but the polenta was not right. I was really sweating until I got the idea to pump the polenta through a pastry bag onto a sheet pan so they would all look like the top of your cappuccino — like a puff — then bake them. When we served them, the James Beard people said this was one of the best polentas they'd ever tasted. It was a discovery based on a mistake!

And oh my god, the quail. We'd asked for the jumbo quail from Oregon and instead got the smallest Jenny-Craig-diet quail I'd ever seen! I stuffed them with Ellensburg lamb sausage. When they came out of the oven they looked like little bodybuilders all pumped up. But when they were cut open, the heartiness of the sausage made up for the size of the birds; it was wonderful.

About 60 people flew in from Seattle for the dinner, all my good friends, my customers. I call them the "good fellas." It really made me feel loved. And to have everything turn out the way it did! The bottom line is that if I die tomorrow, I have had it all.

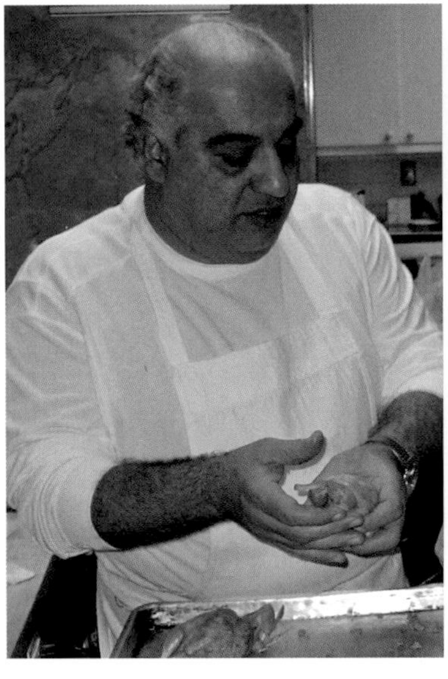

Quaglia Ripiena
STUFFED QUAIL

3 slices artisan bread, crust removed
1 cup milk
12 ounces mild Italian bulk sausage
1 egg
1 teaspoon salt, plus more for seasoning
1/2 teaspoon freshly ground black pepper
3 teaspoons chopped fresh Italian parsley
4 medium to large whole quail, cleaned
1/2 cup flour
1 1/2 tablespoons olive oil
4 thin slices prosciutto
Red Wine Sauce with Sage

Preheat oven to 375°F.

Soak bread slices in milk in a medium bowl for 5 minutes; discard milk.

In a large bowl, combine bread, sausage, egg, 1 teaspoon salt, pepper, and 1 teaspoon parsley. Knead thoroughly with your hands and form into 4 balls about the same size as the quail.

Carefully stuff each quail. You may not need all of the stuffing. Place stuffed quail on a plate, sprinkle with salt, and coat lightly with flour.

In a medium sauté pan, heat 1 tablespoon olive oil over medium-high heat. Sear quail for about 1 minute, rotate a quarter turn and sear for another minute, and repeat until quail are light gold on all sides, about 4 minutes. Set the pan aside for making the sauce.

Place quail, breast side up, on a 12-by-18-inch sheet pan or cookie sheet with edges. Wrap each quail in 1 slice of prosciutto, tucking the ends under the quail. Drizzle remaining 1/2 tablespoon olive oil over the quail and bake for 25 minutes.

Meanwhile, prepare the Red Wine Sauce with Sage.

When the quail are done, remove to a platter, place a sprig of sage from the sauce on top of each one, and spoon the sauce evenly over the quail. Sprinkle with remaining parsley and serve immediately.

Serves 4.

Salsa di Vino Rosso e Salvia

RED WINE SAUCE WITH SAGE

1 tablespoon olive oil
1 tablespoon minced fresh garlic
1/2 teaspoon salt
1/2 teaspoon freshly ground pepper
4 fresh sage leaves
1 cup red table wine
1 cup veal or beef broth (see recipe, page 57)
1/3 cup heavy cream

Add olive oil to the pan used to sear the quail. Bring to medium heat and add garlic, salt, pepper, and sage. Sauté until garlic and sage begin to turn golden brown, about 3 minutes.

Add wine and broth, bring to a boil, and cook for 4 minutes, or until reduced by half. Add cream and cook over medium-low heat for 4 minutes. Keep warm until you are ready to serve.

Barbaresco
Meritage

Petti di Pollo Trifolati
SAUTÉED CHICKEN BREASTS

2 tablespoons olive oil
4 boneless chicken breast halves
8 ounces crimini mushrooms, cleaned and sliced
1/2 cup brandy
1 teaspoon Dijon mustard
2 cups heavy cream
2 tablespoons finely chopped fresh Italian parsley
Freshly ground black pepper (no salt, please)

Heat oil in a large sauté pan over medium heat. Pan-sear chicken, about 4 minutes per side. Add mushrooms and sauté for another 6 minutes. Reduce heat and simmer for 10 minutes. Add brandy, mustard, and cream. Stir and simmer for 10 minutes, or until reduced by half. Sprinkle with parsley and black pepper to taste.

Serves 4.

Montepulciano
Cabernet Franc

Pollo Blu
CHICKEN BREASTS WITH GORGONZOLA

2 tablespoons olive oil
4 boneless chicken breast halves
1/2 cup dry white wine
6 ounces Gorgonzola cheese, diced
1 pint heavy cream
2 tablespoons finely chopped fresh Italian parsley
Freshly ground black pepper (no salt, please)

Preheat oven to 375°F.

Heat oil in a medium ovenproof sauté pan over medium heat. Pan-sear chicken, about 4 minutes per side. Reduce heat, add wine, and simmer for 10 minutes. Stir in Gorgonzola and then cream. Place in the oven for 15 minutes, or until the cream has been reduced. Sprinkle with parsley and black pepper to taste.

Serves 4.

Roero Arneis
Semillon

Pollo Mattone

TERRA-COTTA CHICKEN

1 tablespoon olive oil, plus more for garnish
1 chicken (about 3 1/2 pounds)
Coarse-grained salt
Freshly ground black pepper
1 large sprig fresh rosemary or 1 tablespoon fresh rosemary leaves preserved in salt or dried and blanched

Place the top (heavy) part of a terra-cotta mattone* over a burner covered with a flame-tamer.** Lightly oil the bottom part and place it over a second burner covered with a flame-tamer. Heat the 2 parts over medium heat for at least 15 minutes; they must be very hot.

Meanwhile, cut chicken completely through the breast, open it up, and pound so it will lie flat when placed between the 2 pieces of terra-cotta. Sprinkle a large pinch of salt over the bottom of the mattone; place chicken on it. Sprinkle chicken with a little more salt, a little pepper, and rosemary; cover with the mattone top. Cook for about 40 minutes over medium-low heat, turning the chicken about every 10 minutes. The chicken will be crisp and very juicy. If desired, drip a little olive oil over the chicken before serving.

Serves 4.

Gavi di Gavi
Riesling

This dish goes well with roasted potatoes and a mixed salad.

**A mattone (the Italian word for brick) is a two-part terra-cotta press that can be found in kitchen stores.*

***A flame-tamer is a steel plate that is placed on top of a stove burner to distribute and diffuse the heat evenly. Flame-tamers can be found in kitchen stores or online.*

Passera di Mare all'Acqua Pazza

HALIBUT WITH FENNEL AND TOMATOES

4 tablespoons olive oil
1 garlic clove, minced
1 sprig fresh rosemary
1 teaspoon red pepper flakes
1 fennel bulb, cut into 1/2-inch cubes
2 ripe tomatoes, diced
1/2 cup dry white wine
1 cup fish broth (see recipe, page 60)
1 cup marinara (see recipe, page 81)
4 8-ounce fresh halibut fillets
Salt
Freshly ground black pepper

In a 6-quart soup pot, heat olive oil over medium heat until it begins to smoke. Add garlic, rosemary, red pepper flakes, and fennel; cook until soft and light golden brown, about 8 to 10 minutes. Add tomatoes, wine, fish broth, and marinara; bring to a boil. Reduce heat to low and simmer for 10 minutes. Add halibut and salt and pepper to taste; simmer until cooked through, about 5 minutes.

Carefully pour into a soup tureen. Serve with plenty of freshly ground black pepper and grilled Tuscan bread.

Serves 4.

Chardonnay
Sauvignon Blanc

Salmone al Cartoccio

SALMON IN PARCHMENT

Parchment paper
2 garlic cloves, minced
2 tablespoons fresh lemon juice
1/3 cup chopped fresh Italian parsley
1 dash red pepper flakes
1/2 cup extra-virgin olive oil
Salt
Freshly ground black pepper
1 lemon
4 pieces center-cut salmon fillet, 6 to 7 ounces each, 1/2 to 1 1/2 inches thick (with or without skin)

Preheat oven to 350°F. Prepare four 12- to 15-inch square pieces of parchment paper.

In a small bowl, combine garlic, lemon juice, parsley, red pepper flakes, olive oil, and salt and pepper to taste; mix well. Cut the lemon in half lengthwise, then crosswise to make 12 to 16 half-moon slices.

Place salmon on the parchment paper and arrange 3 to 4 lemon slices on each fillet. Cover with 2 tablespoons of marinade. Fold the parchment paper over the salmon and fold the edges to seal. Place on a baking sheet and bake for 25 to 30 minutes. The cases will swell up during cooking and be full of steam when removed from the oven. Carefully cut the paper in fourths and fold back to remove the salmon. Place on a serving dish and serve immediately.

Dolcetto
Pinot Noir

Serves 4.

7
Dolce

I'm a cheese fanatic. I'm a mouse. I love cheeses. Naturally, every once in a while you've got to have a tiramisu or panna cotta for dessert, so I have included those important recipes here. But I encourage you to get into the habit of serving a small selection of cheeses for dessert. Italians have fewer cavities than Americans because Italians often end the meal with a little cheese rather than loading up on sugary desserts. The enzymes in artisan cheese help protect the teeth.

I have heard Americans say they are too full for cheese after a meal. There is a misconception that to have a cheese plate means eating half a pound of cheese. No! The cheese plate should have very small portions of cheese balanced with a small slice of fruit or a teaspoon of preserves. It's not about one last course to make sure you are full. It is a palate shift that signals the end of a wonderful meal and provides a foil for a delicious dessert wine. This also makes an enjoyable evening around the table last longer.

There are three very important elements to serving cheese after a meal, and you can't do without any of them: the wine, the cheese, and the fruit or nut. There are many variations you can try, but in each case, put some thought into how those three elements go together.

You know me by now, so it's no surprise that first I choose the wine! If I'm going to have a heavy red wine, I feature sharp cheeses, especially blue cheese. If I choose a Pinot Grigio or a Chardonnay, I focus on creamy cheeses. You want to balance it. A heavier wine calls for a more flavorful cheese, but you don't want to overpower the flavor of the wine. When you get into Port wines, the possibilities are endless. When you balance the three elements just right, it's a marriage of love with every sip.

How do I select the cheeses for Assaggio? I go to the creamery, sit down with the cheesemakers, open a bottle of wine, and spend an enjoyable afternoon. It's the only way I can be sure that you will have the same experience when you sit down at my table.

Cheese tastes even better when accompanied by seasonal fruit, nuts, and wine. Here are some suggestions:

Fruit

In summer, serve fresh fruit such as strawberries, grapes, peaches, pears, apples, or figs. Honey is a nice garnish in warmer weather.

In winter, use dried fruit such as apricots and dates.

Nuts

Serve pistachios, walnuts, almonds, and hazelnuts.

Wine

In general, I prefer lighter wines with lighter cheeses in warmer weather and full-bodied reds with more assertive cheeses when it's cold.

Cheese:	Sharp/Blue Vein	Medium	Mild
Wine:	*Amarone*	*Vin Santo*	*Franciacorta*
	Zinfandel	*Port*	*Sparkling*
		Late Harvest	*Prosecco*
			Moscato
			Late Harvest

These are real people
following their passion.
You can taste it.

The number of quality artisan creameries in the United States making great cheeses grows every year. But you won't find many of their products in your local grocery. Specialty, gourmet, and high-end groceries are beginning to stock regional artisan cheeses, but you have to search for them. It's worth it! Good cheese comes only from good milk. The best artisan cheesemakers have a select herd of cows, goats, or sheep that are fed with only natural, organic feed.

Many of the cheeses I serve at Assaggio come from Rogue Creamery and Vella Cheese. I spent a lot of time finding these cheesemakers, getting to know their specialties, and making sure they have a passion for what they do. Both creameries were started by the Vella family after they emigrated from Italy in the 1920s, bringing with them an expertise in handcrafted cheese.

Today, Ignazio Vella is the godfather of artisan cheesemaking. He is truly passionate about what he does. His Sonoma creamery produces a *mezzo secco* (partially dry) Jack and a Toma that are both award-winning, delicious cheeses. Cheesemakers David Gremmels and Cary Bryant of Rogue Creamery have taken blue cheese to a whole new level. Their Oregonzola and Crater Lake Blue are fantastic dessert cheeses. I insist on honest, simple cooking with the freshest ingredients. I apply the same rule to the cheeses I serve.

Rogue Creamery Photography: Rob Rebman

Fragole al Balsamico

BALSAMIC STRAWBERRIES

1/4 cup sweet Marsala
1/2 cup balsamic vinegar
1/4 cup sugar
1 teaspoon grated orange zest
1 teaspoon fresh lemon juice
2 pints strawberries, hulled and quartered
6 fresh mint leaves

In a saucepan, combine Marsala, vinegar, sugar, grated orange zest, and lemon juice; boil for 8 minutes. Add strawberries, remove from the heat, and stir. Let cool for 10 minutes. Garnish with mint leaves and serve.

Serves 6.

Vin Santo
Late Harvest Riesling or Semillon yum!

6/4/10— Good but 8 min might be too long— quickly turns to candy!

Tiramisu

1 quart heavy cream
4 ounces cream cheese, softened
4 ounces mascarpone*
1 1/2 cups sugar
4 eggs
3 cups brewed coffee
1/2 cup sweet Marsala
1 cup brewed espresso
1 14-ounce package ladyfingers
Cocoa powder

In a bowl, combine heavy cream, cream cheese, mascarpone, 1 cup sugar, and eggs for the cream layer. Set aside.

In another bowl, combine coffee, Marsala, espresso, and 1/2 cup sugar. Dip each ladyfinger individually in the coffee mixture, soaking for a few seconds, and then place in a single layer in a 9-by-11-inch (or 10-by-10-inch) glass pan with 2- to 3-inch sides. Add a 2-inch layer of cream mixture. Add another layer of soaked ladyfingers. Add another 2-inch layer of cream mixture. Smooth the surface. Sprinkle with cocoa powder.

Cover with plastic wrap and refrigerate for 24 hours. Cut and serve.

Serves 6 to 8.

Moscato
Port

**Mascarpone is Italian cream cheese. The Galbani brand is available at most high-end grocery stores.*

Panna Cotta

COOKED CREAM

3 1/4 cups confectioners' sugar
2 cups heavy cream
1 cup whole milk
6 teaspoons unflavored gelatin
1 cup raspberries, blueberries, or strawberries
(or a mixture), cleaned and hulled
1 to 2 tablespoons granulated sugar

Combine confectioners' sugar, cream, and milk in a heavy saucepan; cook over medium-high heat, stirring constantly. Remove the pan from the heat just as the contents begin to bubble; do not boil. Drizzle in gelatin, stirring constantly. Continue stirring for 5 minutes, then pour into a bowl. Stir occasionally while the mixture cools.

When the custard is cold, pour into 4 to 6 ramekins. Refrigerate for at least 8 hours or preferably overnight.

To prepare the topping, combine berries with granulated sugar in a small bowl and let stand for at least 30 minutes and preferably for 1 to 2 hours.

When ready to serve, fill a small skillet with enough water to reach about halfway up the side of a ramekin; bring the water to a simmer. Use a knife to loosen the custard from the sides of the ramekins. Place each ramekin in the skillet for 1 to 2 seconds and then invert onto an individual serving plate, shaking gently to unmold. Just before serving, spoon berries over each custard.

Serves 4 to 6.

Moscato
Late Harvest Riesling

8
Vino

I don't want to tell you your business, but you really have to drink wine with food of passion. And don't wait until dinner is served. A glass of wine should be right there on the kitchen counter next to all of your fresh ingredients. Food of passion is not complete without wine that goes with it to provide the spark.

Americans have to loosen up about wine. Embrace the Italian culture. In Italy, when you go to lunch you have a glass of wine; it's just a natural fact. Water, juice, tea — they all cost more than wine anyway. It's not about finishing a whole bottle or "drinking" during the day. No. One glass is a God-given, from the earth, made by growers and winemakers with passion, mandatory right. Come to your table, enjoy. That's it.

When I discuss wines with my staff at the restaurant, you'd better believe we are tasting wine. You can't just tell people how to talk about wine, what words to use. That's cheating. To me, if you are talking about wine, you'd better drink wine. My seven-year-old daughter, Francesca, can tell the difference between individual Chardonnays by nose and taste. It's not difficult — you just need to practice.

For most of the recipes in this cookbook I have made two wine suggestions: one Italian and one from the Pacific Northwest. Italian wine is an excellent match for my cooking, but the truth is, Washington and Oregon growers are now producing wines that go perfectly with food of passion. The wine pairings recommended here are combinations that balance well. That's the only way to really know what food might go with what wine. You have to try it out. There are certainly other wines that will work with any particular dish, but have a backup ready in case the combination doesn't balance. If your wine overpowers your dish, don't be afraid to move to a more subtle wine; you can finish that more intense wine with your pork with balsamic reduction tomorrow. You could even open both and let your guests help decide which one to serve. That is what food of passion is all about.

It's about
you and me
with a few
friends, at home,
drinking wine,
getting happy,
and cooking.

Grazie

To all my patrons, thank you. You began as my customers, but through the passion of food you have become my friends. With this cookbook, my spirit is going to be in your home cooking with you.

From my soul I want to thank my executive chef, Iram Macias. We have been through so much together that he is a part of me. Iram has put so much energy and time into this cookbook, testing and perfecting these recipes to make sure that my food will work its magic in your home.

Petyr Beck tasted and re-tasted everything. He was our guinea pig. He came into the kitchen with his scale and measuring cups and asked every question he could think of so that you will have success at home.

Thanks also to Kristen Johnson, my general manager and the wine muse for this cookbook, for her creative pairings and for all her insights; Iris Gannon, my assistant, for her hard work and for being my voice to our publisher; and my whole crew at Assaggio, for being behind this project and making the Assaggio experience happen.

My suppliers make it possible to use the freshest ingredients. I go to Pike Place Market to shop every day. We are so blessed to live in the Pacific Northwest, where we have the freshest and finest fish. My fish supplier is my best friend. He came to Francesca's birthday, and I went to his daughter's wedding. We send each other Christmas gifts. My meat purveyor and bread baker, same thing. They are all my good friends.

I especially want to thank my beautiful wife, Karen, and my wonderful daughter, Francesca, because they allow me to go to work and spend time making this cookbook, and they understand how much a part of me it is. Francesca was my special inspiration. I want her to be proud of this book so she can show it to her friends and to her kids and say, "This is from my father." My dream is that she will be either a winemaker or a chef. I know she will be great at anything she does. She is the future that inspires me.

Index